Routes of
Cross-Cultural
Exchange

The Panama Canal

Tatiana Ryckman

Cavendish
Square
New York

Published in 2018 by Cavendish Square Publishing, LLC
243 5th Avenue, Suite 136, New York, NY 10016

First Edition

CPSIA Compliance Information: Batch #CS17CSQ

All websites were available and accurate when this book was sent to press.
Library of Congress Cataloging-in-Publication Data

Names: Ryckman, Tatiana, author.
Title: The Panama Canal / Tatiana Ryckman.
Description: New York : Cavendish Square Publishing, 2018. | Series: Routes of cross-cultural exchange | Includes bibliographical references and index.
Identifiers: LCCN 2016055205 (print) | LCCN 2016056163 (ebook) | ISBN 9781502626929 (library bound) | ISBN 9781502626783 (E-book)
Subjects: LCSH: Panama Canal (Panama)--History--Juvenile literature. | Canals--Panama--Design and construction--History--Juvenile literature. | Canal Zone--History--Juvenile literature.
Classification: LCC F1569.C2 R95 2018 (print) | LCC F1569.C2 (ebook) | DDC 972.87--dc23
LC record available at https://lccn.loc.gov/2016055205

Editorial Director: David McNamara
Editor: Caitlyn Miller
Copy Editor: Alex Tessman
Associate Art Director: Amy Greenan
Designer: Jessica Nevins
Production Coordinator: Karol Szymczuk
Photo Research: J8 Media

The photographs in this book are used by permission and through the courtesy of: Cover Alfredo Maiquez/Lonely Planet Images/Getty Images; p. 5 Biberbaer/Wikimedia Commons/File:Ship Providence Bay at panama canal.jpg/CC PD; p. 8 Peter Hermes Furian/Shutterstock.com; p. 11 Christian Strassnig/Wikimedia Commons/File:Camino Real close the shore of Alajuela Lake.jpg/ CC BY-SA 3.0; p. 16 Kean Collection/Archive Photos/Getty Images; p. 19 Everett Historical/ Shutterstock.com; p. 22 PongMoji/Shutterstock.com; p. 27 Universal History Archive/Universal Images Group/Getty Images; p. 32 Yuri_Arcurs/iStock; p. 37 bikeriderlondon/Shutterstock.com; p. 38 tzooka/iStock/Thinkstock; p. 40 Wally McNamee/Corbis Historical/Getty Images; p. 43 Etienne Carjat/Hulton Archive/Getty Images; p. 47 Bob Thomas/Popperfoto/Getty Images; p. 51 Time Life Pictures/The LIFE Images Collection/Getty Images; p. 54, 72 Bettmann/Getty Images; p. 56 John van Hasselt/Sygma/Getty Images; p. 60 Michael Maslan/Corbis Historical/Getty Images; p. 68 ANGEL MURILLO/AFP/Getty Images; p. 74 RODRIGO ARANGUA/AFP/Getty Images; p. 77 MCT/Newscom; p. 81 epa European pressphoto agency b.v./Alamy Stock Photo; p. 83 Vintagepix/ Shutterstock.com; p. 85 Liz O.Baylen/Los Angeles Times/Getty Images.

Printed in the United States of America

Table of Contents

Introduction

The Legacy of the Panama Canal

The Panama Canal has played an enormous role in creating our modern global trade economy. At the time of its construction, the Panama Canal provided a faster, safer route from the Atlantic Ocean to the Pacific for the ships and crews that transported goods from all over the world. A faster route also meant a cheaper route because fewer provisions and man hours were needed to make the same trip. Seen as a feat of engineering genius, the canal has become responsible for transferring 5 percent of the world's shipping. Nearly 90 percent of the world's goods are still transported via **maritime** commerce, or traded by sea.

From the first glimmer of hope for a canal to its completion in 1914, nearly five hundred years passed. Five nations had attempted a trade route through the area in this time. Panama itself had made two important plays for independence.

An estimated twenty-seven thousand workers died in the construction of the canal from the

Ships moving through the Panama Canal's original locks can carry as many as five thousand containers.

dangerous work, disease, or from violence that broke out between natives and **expatriates** (foreigners who came to Panama looking for work). The Panama Canal is an impressive testament to the muscle and engineering brilliance of America at that time. However, like many other historic monuments of powerful civilizations, it was built at the expense of thousands of people whose names we'll never know.

Before the canal, the Isthmus of Panama—that narrow strip of land connecting Mexico to South America—was part of a confederation of Central and South American states. This confederation had only recently broken away from Spanish rule. As Colombia (then Granada) gained power and influence over the confederation, Panama sought to break away from yet another coercive government. With the aid of the United States, Panama declared independence once again in 1903. Panamanians found themselves controlled by yet another foreign power—America.

Even with the political turmoil that accompanied the building of the canal, the people and government of Panama welcomed this manmade marvel to their homeland. The canal promised money, trade, growth, and culture. And the canal delivered on that promise—eventually.

More than fifty years after its completion, United States President Jimmy Carter signed a treaty in 1977 with Panamanian dictator Omar Torrijos. This agreement promised the rights to the canal to Panama by the end of the twentieth century. In 1999, the Panamanian government was finally able to enjoy full control of the canal that was built through their own country.

In 2016, Panama completed a massive update to the canal that took ten years and required forty thousand workers. Over the last hundred years, ships have grown to carry more cargo. These new ships are twice as large as the **Panamax** ships, which were built to the specifications of the original canal for the last 100 years. Unable to fit the new ships though the original **locks** of the canal, the canal had to expand.

In order to accommodate the new ships, the Panama Canal has added an additional lane that has the potential to move three times the amount of cargo of the original canal, which is also still in operation. But the influence of this new, massive expansion does not just affect Panama. The reason for building the canal over 100 years ago was to improve world trade.

This update means ports all over the world—especially along the East Coast of the United States, have had to prepare to receive the new, larger ships.

In New York and New Jersey, Port Authority has spent $6 billion in renovations that will allow them to accept the new ships. Updates include actually removing earth from the bottom of the ocean to make the port deeper, as well as building storage facilities for the additional cargo that will be dropped off.

The bigger ships also mean new kinds of goods can travel along the famous canal. Products that are usually transported on larger ships, like natural gas, can now move more quickly through the expanded canal.

Just as the original canal created controversy, the new canal also has objectors. Only a few months after the new canal opened, a Chinese ship ran into the wall of the lock. The accident led critics to argue the new design might not be safe. Others have said that with a sagging economy, especially in China where many of the world's products are produced, people aren't buying as much. They claim there isn't a demand for greater shipping volume.

Whether the new locks will have the same impact on the world's trade that the original canal had over 100 years ago remains to be seen. Even so, the importance of the canal in world trade, economics, and politics cannot be denied.

ATLANTIC OCEAN
Caribbean Sea
Colón
Cativá
Limon Bay
Chagres River
Gatun Dam
1
Gatun Locks
PANAMA
Panama Canal
Barro Colorado Isl.
Gatun Lake
Alajuela Lake
Madden Dam
Gamboa
Chagres River
Panama Canal Railway
Panama Canal
PANAMA
2
Pedro Miguel Locks
Miraflores Lake
3
Miraflore
Locks
CITY
Arraiján
0 5 10 15 km
0 2 4 6 8 10 mi

Chapter 1

Trade Before the Panama Canal

Panama is an **isthmus**, or narrow stretch of land, that connects Colombia in South America to Costa Rica in Central America. For hundreds of years, explorers, merchants, and militaries used this narrow land bridge to cross from the Pacific Ocean to the Atlantic. As a result, the people of Panama itself were ruled by a series of outside governments.

Early Life on the Isthmus

Ancient cultures on the Panama isthmus were hunter-gathers who lived in temporary structures, such as caves. The earliest artifacts suggest humans have lived in the area since 8000 BCE. Yet they did not begin to form settlements until thousands of years later, around 5000 BCE. These settlements formed along the coasts, which allowed people to stay in one place as the ocean provided a steady

Opposite: *It took nearly five hundred years to make the Panama Canal (represented here by a red line) a reality.*

supply of food. Tools also became more sophisticated by this time, suggesting a more permanent way of life.

Staying in one place allowed these early populations to pursue craftsmanship, making weaponry, arts, jewelry, and more. These valuable items could be exchanged for goods from other areas, just as countries all over the world trade for unique, regional goods today. Commonly traded items included pearls from the Caribbean, salt from the marshes in the Pacific, shells, and objects made of a gold alloy (called "base gold" by the Spanish, who would soon arrive).

These are the cultures early European explorers would have encountered, including the Spanish explorer Christopher Columbus, who landed on the Isthmus in 1502.

Culture Clash

European colonization was as difficult for isthmus natives as it was for Native Americans when the United States was first settled. Many **indigenous** populations suffered from exposure to new diseases, enslavement, and massacres. Those who survived these horrifying times fled established settlements to live in the forests and nearby islands.

When the native population dwindled and dispersed, the ruling Spaniards bought slaves from Nicaragua to replace the Panamanians, charging only 5 pesos per slave. It was the Spaniards who first envisioned a canal through Panama. However, the technology for building one did not yet exist. Instead, early European settlers worked to establish an over-ground trade route through the difficult terrain of the isthmus. From 1526 to 1563, Spain deported more than 99,000 Nicaraguans to Panama. The practice

Today the Camino Real is used as a hiking trail in the dry season, when the waters that ordinarily flood it have been diverted to fill the canal.

was finally banned when leaders in Spain learned of a ship where 350 slaves died out of 400 who had been on board. Because the mortality rate was so high, and some slaves were able to escape home over land, the Panamanian population didn't grow with the importation of new slaves. The total population increased to only 29,000—roughly the size of a small American college town.

Despite the environmental challenges and the lack of a labor force, Spain managed to build two roads. One was an 8 foot (2.4 meter) wide, cobble-stone road that extended from Panama City on the Atlantic Ocean to Cruces on the Chagres River. This road facilitated the transportation of goods to the Pacific. Travelers on this route often fell prey to pirates, though. And these incidents meant losing valuable cargo. The other, much more difficult road passed through mountains, crossed two major rivers, and narrowed in places to only 3 feet (.9 m) wide with 500 foot (152 m) drops on either side. This road was known as the Camino Real. It took four days for a party of twenty-four trained slaves to guide 1,200 mules carrying 200 pounds (90.7 kilograms) each to make the journey.

One of the most important goods traded via these new routes was Peruvian silver, which Spain collected from Peru as a "mining tax" for extracting the silver. Some of the most frequently traded goods were textiles, wine, and oil. Carrying on its new tradition of slave labor, Panama also became an important avenue for trading slaves from Africa.

The Camino Real was a laborious and dangerous road. It was expensive to use it to trade slaves, too. The price of slaves since the ban on the Nicaraguan slave trade had skyrocketed to 450 pesos per slave. The trip became even more expensive because mule owners were able to charge high prices for the rental of their animals to make the journey. Yet nautical navigation technology improved during this time as well. Gradually merchants chose to sail the extra

8,000 miles (12,874 km) around the entire continent of South America rather than cross the isthmus.

A Moment of Independence

The diverse population of Panama slowly adapted to a European way of life as cities were established and universities built. Spanish became the unifying language. Spain's power expanded in South and Central America for over three hundred years—until those nations were able to establish independence.

As Spain lost power in Europe, it also lost its control over the New World. On November 28, 1821, the Panamanians were at last free of Spanish rule. Meanwhile, to the south, the famous South American military and political leader Simon Bolivar of Venezuela helped unite the South American states against the Spanish. He celebrated the isthmus's declaration of independence.

A few years earlier, in 1815, Bolivar wrote his famous "Jamaica Letter" from exile. He wrote a few lines about the isthmus's unique potential:

> The states of the Isthmus of Panamá as far as Guatemala, will perhaps form a confederation. Because of their magnificent position between two mighty oceans, they may in time become the emporium of the world. Their canals will shorten distances throughout the world, strengthen commercial ties between Europe, America, and Asia, and bring to that happy area tribute from the four quarters of the globe. There some day, perhaps, the capital of the world may be located.

Dangers Around the Horn

Prior to the construction of the canal, ships had to take a long, dangerous route around the horn of South America. The seas of the Drake Passage, the body of water between South America and the islands off Antarctica, are especially violent. Chad Greene, a glaciologist at the University of Texas, says, "[Strong winds] drive the Antarctic Circumpolar Current (ACC), which is a continuous ocean current that flows clockwise all around Antarctica. The ACC has a higher flowrate than all the world's rivers combined, about equivalent to five thousand Amazon Rivers. But it's the wind that causes the choppiest seas in the world."

This route was referred to as the Manila galleon route, named after the Spanish ships that traveled from Acapulco in Mexico to Manila in the Philippines. Previous traders between Europe and China had traveled above land across the Middle East or by sailing around Africa. This new route, however, allowed the Spaniards to collect goods from Mexico and South America along the way.

In 1898, the USS *Oregon* had to travel this route—a journey totaling 50,000 miles (80,467.2 km) that took more than two months—in order to reinforce American troops in Cuba during the Spanish-American War. The American people tracked the progress of the ship throughout its long journey, worried for the soldiers on board, the soldiers in Cuba who awaited reinforcements, and America's future. This tense voyage further convinced the future president, Theodore Roosevelt (who was only a soldier in Cuba at the time), of the value of a canal that would provide a faster, safer route from the West Coast to the East Coast.

In the short term, Bolivar was correct that a confederation would form. In the long term, he was correct that a canal would draw commercial enterprises through the region. But he was not able to predict at what cost.

Convinced that Bolivar would help lead them to a bright future, the isthmus joined Venezuela and New Granada (today's Colombia) as each nation worked toward developing new independent governments. Yet hundreds of years of Spanish influence made different impressions in different regions. Just as there were growing pains when America decided to break away from Great Britain, in South America, some citizens and officials were still loyal to Spain. Others wanted to break away completely. These tensions led to cracks. Over the subsequent seventy years, the isthmus left and rejoined the confederation.

Chapter 2

Foundations and Explorations

The events leading to the construction of the Panama Canal were as long and winding as the trade route the canal was meant to replace. Over the course of hundreds of years, at least five nations sent expeditions to South and Central America seeking a shortcut from the Atlantic to the Pacific Ocean.

Whose Route Is It Anyway?

The first spark of an idea for a canal that would cut through Panama came to Charles V, Holy Roman Emperor and King of Spain, in 1534. He sent a **convoy** to survey the Americas for an alternate route that would save his ships valuable time and money as they traveled from Spain to Peru, on the western side of South America.

Opposite: *Christopher Columbus first arrived in Panama in 1502; by 1532, Spain began looking for a way to cut through the isthmus.*

Without the infrastructure, man power, or technology to build a canal in the 1500s, Charles V opted for other trade routes. These routes involved crossing the isthmus over land and circumventing all of South America.

Other nations made attempts at cutting trade routes through the narrow land strip connecting the Atlantic and Pacific oceans. In 1698, the Kingdom of Scotland made an ill-fated attempt at an over-land trade route called the Darien Scheme. Due to a lack of funding and the challenges of the terrain, the route was abandoned by 1700.

In 1788, more than 250 years after Charles V's original survey, Thomas Jefferson (then an ambassador to France) advocated for the Spanish construction of a canal in Panama. Even at that early date, Jefferson saw that a canal would be an advantage to American trade. He also believed that the Spanish who had surveyed the area refused to build a canal for fear that it would be a greater advantage to the United States than their own country.

In 1843, the British began making plans for a canal in the area. They even entered into a contract with the Republic of Granada. That plan was called the Atlantic and Pacific Canal. It was projected to be completed in an ambitious five years, but again, nothing came of it.

The discovery of gold in California in 1849 led the United States to seek faster, safer, and cheaper ways of getting from the East Coast to the West. The Panama Railway was built by American businessmen who saw the opportunity to make a profit on travelers going west to pan for gold. The railroad would later be a huge asset in the building of the canal.

The Panama Railroad was a precursor to the Panama Canal and proved invaluable when canal construction began.

The Panama Railroad and the Cadaver Trade

America's trans-continental railroad would prove invaluable when excavation began on the canal. It provided an efficient way to cart laborers, materials, and tourists through the Canal Zone. Building the railroad proved both treacherous and lucrative. As many as ten thousand workers died from disease and dangerous jobs.

The exact number of fatalities on the railroad is difficult to estimate because of poor record keeping. Laborers from all over the world, including the United States, China, Africa, and the Caribbean, arrived with no identification and were known to their fellow workers by only a first name. One of the major obstacles of the construction of the railroad became figuring out what to do with all the bodies.

Because much of the land covered by the 47 miles (75.6 km) of track were swampy, workers couldn't be buried until crews reached higher ground. This challenge, combined with the high death toll, led to the Panama Cadaver Trade. Medical schools and hospitals needed **cadavers** for medical students to practice on, so schools would pay for bodies that had been preserved (some say "pickled") in barrels. The money this new trade earned went to running the isthmus's own hospital as doctors tried to cure patients of malaria and yellow fever. This was a losing battle, however, as it would take another forty years before the connection between these tropical diseases and the mosquito was discovered.

The lack of a cure for diseases and inability to prevent people from contracting them meant the cadaver trade would continue to boom until the completion of the rail road.

In 1869, the same year construction was completed on the Suez Canal, President Ulysses S. Grant sent an American fleet to look for a new route from the Atlantic to the Pacific. Though it was a priority throughout his presidency, the project never happened. In 1875, a team of American surveyors were again sent to Panama in search of a new route. The team decided Panama was too expensive and suggested a twelve-lock canal in Nicaragua instead.

Finally, in 1879, construction on the canal began. under Ferdinand de Lesseps, a French politician who had just completed work on the impressive Suez Canal in Egypt. After hundreds of years of surveys and planning, the canal would finally become a reality.

The French Canal

Ferdinand de Lesseps's plan for a sea-level canal through Panama was approved in 1879. The French-sponsored canal began construction later that year. The estimated cost of the project was 1.2 billion francs, or 240 million dollars (adjusted for **inflation** the French canal would cost 5.7 billion dollars today). The project was projected to come in under budget and take only six years. His reputation after building the Suez Canal convinced investors to trust de Lesseps with much of their wealth.

But de Lesseps was not an engineer, and the canal never came to be as he imagined it. Many experts believe the primary challenge to de Lesseps's plan was his insistence on a sea-level canal. This meant that everything from the swamps to the mountains would have to be made the same height as the ocean. Excavation on the project was slow and dangerous. Illnesses, such as malaria and yellow fever, and heavy

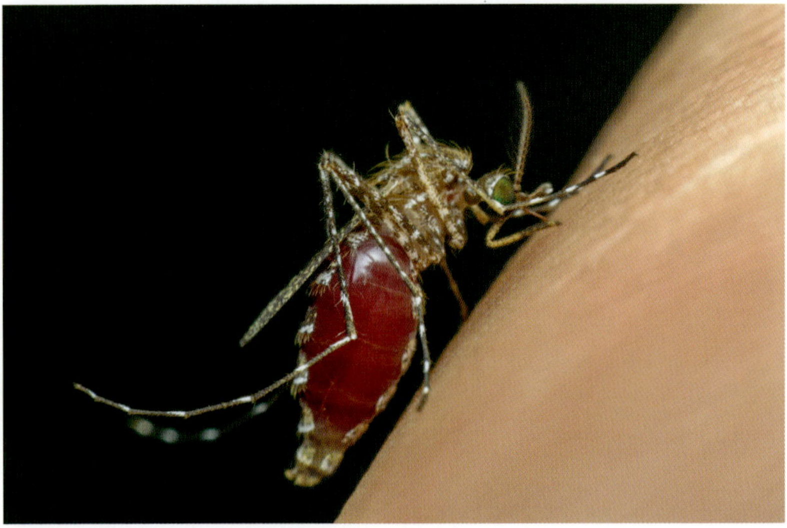

Mosquitos were found to be the culprits behind the massive malaria and yellow fever deaths in Panama. Yet during de Lesseps's management, little was done to resolve the issue

rains that caused deadly landslides were just two of the obstacles the French faced. Finally, the project went bankrupt.

After nine years and excavating less than half of the canal, the French stopped their efforts. Yet one positive development came from it all. De Lesseps had hired a doctor to help control the spread of tropical diseases. It was this physician, Dr. Carlos Finlay, who discovered the connection between mosquitos and disease. Finlay's theory was well received in the medical community. However, de Lesseps did little to address the mosquito population and thousands of people lost their lives. An estimated twenty thousand people died during the period of French work, many of them poor West Indians and Caribbean natives who hoped to make a living they could send back to their families. De Lesseps himself, though an accomplished businessman, returned home defeated.

A Feat of American Engineering

Today the canal is seen as one of the seven engineering wonders of the world. The electric lock system lifts enormous shipping vessels 85 feet (25.9 m) into Lake Gatun—the largest manmade lake for decades, covering 160 square miles (414 square kilometers)—before lowering ships back down the other side. But this world wonder did not build itself. Faced with the same issues that plagued the French construction, the American engineers worked in phases over a span of ten years. They gradually made the dream of a canal across the isthmus a reality.

Legacy and Logistics

In *The Big Ditch, How American Took, Built, Ran, and Ultimately Gave Away the Panama Canal*, Noel Maurer and Carlos Yu write:

> From a distance, in North America, the Panama Canal seems like … a historical leftover from a discreditable and nearly forgotten chapter of US history. Up close, however, it is immediately apparent that the Panama Canal is one of the world's great waterways, the highly efficient economic engine for a rather prosperous Latin American country. Both of these interpretations of the Panama Canal are correct.

In other words, the canal was seen as part of America's **imperialism**, or domination of other countries. On the other hand, it was as a symbol of American ingenuity.

The United States had just engaged in a questionable and bloody war with the Philippines (in which six hundred thousand Pilipino civilians died). And the French had failed in their attempt to build a canal. Therefore, there were many American citizens and politicians who opposed building a canal through the isthmus of Panama. It was President Theodore Roosevelt who pursued the canal and lobbied tirelessly for its construction. The canal promised to improve trade around the entire world—not just for the US. President Roosevelt convinced Congress and to the American public of the nation's duty to help mankind enter a new global era.

Political "Scheming"

After the assassination of President William McKinley, Vice President Roosevelt was made the thirty-sixth president of the United States. He was known for being a man of adventure. And the construction of a canal that would change world trade forever was exactly the sort of legacy President Roosevelt hoped for.

Congress was on the verge of passing a proposal to build a canal through Nicaragua based on surveys that suggested it would be a safer project. Then a French investor in the original canal, Philippe-Jean Bunau-Varilla, saw an opportunity to recoup some of his losses in the French project. He hired a successful New York lawyer to lobby members of Congress while he himself gave lectures on the benefits of a canal through Panama. President Roosevelt was won to their side, and eventually Congress was convinced. In a vote between the two plans, Panama won by a narrow margin. Those who voted against the "scheme" labeled the Panama Canal plan as corruption.

Even after the decision was made to build a canal through the isthmus, the United States had to secure the rights to build the canal. Initially Roosevelt and the United States government sought a contract with Colombia, the nation that led the confederation of South American states. They negotiated with a Colombian representative in Washington to pay $40 million to build the canal with the right to lease the canal property in **perpetuity** from Colombia. When the contract returned to Colombia, however, their government would not accept the offer. At the same time, Panama wanted to regain their independence and break from the confederation.

The United States quickly shifted positions to assist Panama's liberation movement in hopes that the Panamanian government would agree to the canal project. The Colombian government was no match for the United States's large military, and Panama's road to independence was remarkably smooth. But such generosity was not without expectations. Back in the United States, public opinion was not in Roosevelt's favor. The *New York Times* reported on the events, calling the American involvement in Panama an "act of sordid conquest." Nevertheless, the Republic of Panama became a protectorate of the United States in 1903 after the revolution. The nation remained a protectorate until 1939.

Philippe-Jean Bunau-Varilla became the Panamanian representative to the United States. He agreed to a relatively small sum of money for the United States to control the Canal Zone. Bunau-Varilla owned the rights to assets of the defunct French enterprise, so he stood to benefit from the deal. The United States agreed to pay $10 million and an annual rental fee of $250,000 to Panama. Instead of paying the $10 million directly to the Panamanian government, however, the United States gave $6 million of that to JP Morgan. The famous American banker was to invest the money "on Panama's behalf." The United States then purchased the remaining French equipment (though most of it was in disrepair), the Panama Railroad, and the excavated land from Bunau-Varilla for $40 million.

Thus began the Americans' expensive ten-year construction of the Panama Canal.

Engineering and Industry

American success in Panama is often credited to the system of locks that made it possible to lift ships up and over the mountain range. This system had been used before, but never on such a large scale. There are three locks or "steps" on each side of Gatun Lake, which is the large man-made reservoir at the top of the 85-foot (25.9 m) rise.

Equally impressive is the massive organizational plan that enabled the construction to happen at all. Housing where workers could live had to be built. And some of the most elaborate machine shops in the world at that time were constructed in Panama to fix equipment, build new machines, and maintain parts for the massive electric locks themselves. New machines were invented to aid the enormous number of laborers needed to excavate the land by hand. Other innovations were designed to smooth soil for the massive dam that held back the waters of Lake Gatun.

This photo of President Theodore Roosevelt at the helm of a Bucyrus Digger swept American citizens into a feeling of national pride.

One of the most famous machines invented for the canal was the **Bucyrus digger**, a massive steam-powered shovel that could dig eight tons in a single scoop. The new digging machines quickly out-paced the trains that hauled their dirt away, so additional railroads had to be built to support the project. The shovel itself was used in the railroad improvements because it could easily pick up the tracks and move them. The Bucyrus shovels were built at a plant in Milwaukee, disassembled for shipping, and re-assembled in machine shops in the Canal Zone.

It was a famous picture of President Roosevelt, behind the wheel of this 130,000-pound (58,967 kg) machine that swayed public opinion about the canal project. Roosevelt's trip to the isthmus marked the first time a United States president had left the country while in office. The picture, which circulated widely in newspapers, fit the president's image as a rugged adventurer. The image showed him in a powerful position, controlling the excavation of the canal. It sent a message to Americans that this was the future of the country.

The canal project also represented an enormous amount of work for American citizens who stayed home. Seemingly limitless materials were needed in the building of the canal, and they were all produced in American factories. In addition to the Milwaukee factory for building the Bucyrus digger, the project demanded steel from Pittsburgh, electric parts from General Electric in Boston, and bolts formed in West Virginia.

Ovidio Diaz-Espino, author of *How Wall Street Created a Nation*, said in an interview with PBS that,

"Every lock of the canal, and there are four, has more steel, more concrete, and took more work than the Empire State Building. Something like six Empire State Building constructions are here."

Labor

Before canal workers even arrived on the isthmus, the United States had work to do. The first job was to address the rampant spread of tropical diseases. The link between insects and disease was finally beginning to be accepted. The chief sanitation officer, Colonel William C. Gorgas, immediately set out to eradicate mosquitos. Colonel Gorgas's methods included building modern water systems in cities, eliminating standing water (ideal breeding grounds for mosquitos), covering larger pools of water with insecticide or oil, fumigating buildings, and installing screens in windows and doors.

The buildings themselves had yet to be built. Under French supervision, housing had been abysmal. Many of the workers had lived in tents. Understanding that the project would take many years, the United States placed emphasis on building camps where men could live safely in relative comfort—that is, the white men.

When the canal workers began to show up from the West Indies, the Caribbean, the United States, and Europe, housing was quickly divvied up by race and nationality. The segregation that developed in the Canal Zone began as a division in pay rates. Skilled workers, such as engineers and supervisors brought from the United States to manage the project, were paid in gold US currency. On the other hand, unskilled workers, such as the West Indian men who did the actual digging, were paid in Panamanian silver. Gradually, the United States hired more and more white Americans to fill the higher positions and relied almost entirely on foreign labor for lower-wage jobs. White Americans who came to the canal project with dreams of adventure and the vision of digging out the canal with their own bare hands quickly lost interest after only a few days of back-breaking work. These men looked for other jobs in the Zone. With the exception of local Panamanian workers, nonwhite and non-American workers were almost never considered for higher paying jobs as it was assumed they were more naturally suited to manual labor.

White American men received small houses with window screens while laborers of color were housed in cramped dormitories without screens to protect them from mosquitos. (It was believed that these workers were **immune**, or unable to catch diseases.) The gold and silver payroll was not just a way to segregate housing and income, but also daily life. The YMCA built clubs where "gold employees" could relax, play pool, go bowling, and read. The cafeteria was also segregated, and the quality of food was drastically different for gold and silver workers. Most silver workers were given a sort of slop, which one visitor compared to what he fed his pigs back home. Gold workers enjoyed six weeks' paid vacation so they could return home to the United States to visit their families and "recuperate." Because it was thought that the workers of color would not get sick and did not need to recuperate, they were given only two weeks' paid vacation after they fought for it.

Many of the workers on the silver payroll did die of disease. Unlike the white workers, though, it was often from pneumonia. They did the hardest labor in the worst conditions—often working ten hour days in tropical rain storms. Most were too poor to buy a second set of clothes, so workers would wear the same set of wet, cold clothes for days on end. Sometimes they would sleep in them. This combination was what made them so vulnerable to pneumonia.

Between the French and American efforts, at least twenty-seven thousand people died in the building of the canal (though some estimate the number to be over thirty thousand). It is nearly impossible to imagine human loss on this scale.

The canal was finally opened in 1914, but by then the world had shifted its attention to Europe and the approach of the First World War. Commercial ships didn't begin using the canal until 1920.

UGMU 871696 4
22G1
TRDU 727045 0
22G1
GSTU 592957 6
US 2210
TRDU 727039 0
TRDU 727044 5
22G1
TRDU 727041 9

Chapter 3

Goods and Services

The opening of the Panama Canal provided a much-needed outlet to distribute manufactured goods, which could now be rapidly produced thanks to the **Industrial Revolution**. The Panama Canal made shipping all kinds of products faster, safer, and cheaper. A few businesses in particular seemed to flourish with the opening of this new trade route. Even trade within the United States changed because travel over the vast continent was still slow, difficult, and expensive.

Foreign and Domestic Goods

The United States' lumber industry saw major benefits from the canal. Historically, resources like lumber were sold regionally. But as less expensive transport became available, the markets expanded and distinct varieties of lumber began competing on the national level. The canal made it possible

Opposite: *As industrialization made production easier, industries needed to send their products abroad to larger markets. This was made possible with the Panama Canal.*

to ship Southern pine trees inexpensively. Southern pines began to rival the Douglas firs of the Pacific Northwest. In time, the Northwestern Douglas firs came to be preferred across the nation. Production of Southern soft woods declined, despite their low cost, and Southern businesses suffered while those in the Northwest flourished.

As Noel Maurer and Carlos Yu point out in their book, *The Big Ditch*, there was a significant consequence of the canal's effect on the lumber industry. The president of a Washington timber company, William Boeing, would "[use] his company's profits and aviation-grade timber to start a small airplane company during World War I … By World War II, Boeing had dramatically changed the nature of the Seattle area's economy, with consequences strongly echoed today." Boeing was eventually relocated to Chicago. As of this writing, the company employs roughly 157,000 people.

The opening of the canal also aligned with the California oil boom. Prices for crude oil were dropping in California, where more oil was produced than the state's population could use. The opening of the canal made it possible to ship oil to the East Coast, and the first California oil tanker made the trip in 1922. By the following year, they were shipping as many as 100,000 barrels of oil to the Atlantic coast every day. California's abundance of oil caused them to develop oil-burning technology while the rest of the country continued to rely on coal.

In 1913, John Barrett wrote in his book, *Panama Canal, What It Is, What It Means*, about the canal's potential to bring an industrial boom to the Pacific coast of South and Central America by opening an easier trade route with the United States and Europe:

> I indulge in no foolish or ill-advised prophecy when I predict that the twelve Latin American countries, on their Western shores ... will experience in the decade following the opening of the canal a development of commerce agriculture industry, timber, and mineral wealth, railway construction, harnessing of water-powers, population, cities and towns which will astonish the world.

Barrett's prophecy was, in fact, a little ill-advised. The United States had deliberately blocked Panama's involvement in the canal. Even in the canal's construction, few Panamanians were employed. They were not allowed to sell their goods to the laborers living there (goods from the United States were shipped in and sold exclusively to workers), and Panamanians had few opportunities to sell goods to sailors or tourists on passing ships. Just as Panama failed to see the economic and cultural gains they'd anticipated from the canal, so did the rest of Latin America—with a few exceptions.

With the construction of the canal, other countries in South America were indeed able to trade on the world stage. Chile, for example, was suddenly able to reach a world market for their natural resources. The new route made it inexpensive enough for the nation to trade with the East Coast of the United States. Chile's primary export was iron ore. Their largest mine, El Tofo, alone brought the Chilean government $523 million in royalties, even though the mine was privately owned.

Other countries that had exotic goods, like coffee and chocolate, could more easily trade with northern climates where these delicacies couldn't grow through harsh winters. Barratt also believed that the relationships developed through trade would foster good-will between countries and bring world peace. The forthcoming World Wars, however, suggest that he was wrong about this, too.

Services

Ship Shape

It's easy to focus on the many goods that passed through Panama's gates, but the ships that made the journey became a business in and of themselves. From ship builders to repair shops, and shipping services that delivered goods for other countries, the opportunities presented by the canal seemed limitless.

For years, the Canal Zone boasted the most advanced machine shops and repair equipment. In a "Country Studies" report, published by the Library of Congress, it's noted that shipping-related services flourished in the Canal Zone: "This canal's location at one of the crossroads of international trade has spawned a plethora of other service-oriented activities, such as storage, ship repair, break bulk (the unloading of a portion or all of a ship's cargo), transshipment, bunkering, and distribution and services to ship travelers."

Japan saw the canal as an opportunity to benefit from the business of shipping itself. Between 1914 and 1920, Japan increased its shipping capacity from 5,000 tons to 333,000 tons by expanding its fleet. Elaborate trade patterns were developed so the ships would always be full. Maurer and Yu write that

Coffee was one of a few Central American goods that benefited from the canal's proximity.

"Ships would carry Japanese emigrants to Brazil via the Cape of Good Hope … then transport Brazilian coffee to New Orleans," finally returning to Japan via the Panama Canal with American cotton for use in the Japanese textile industry.

Military Uses

Though Roosevelt had promised the Panama Canal would launch the whole world into an inter-connected economic boom (and it did, sort of), the construction of the canal had been expensive. It would be a long time before the canal would pay itself off. What the canal did immediately provide was a much shorter path for the United States military to travel from one

Tourism

Each year, Panama sees roughly two million tourists who spend an average of $300 US dollars a day visiting the country. Annual profits for tourism are nearly $1.5 million. Tourism can also boost independent businesses and local restaurants that don't otherwise directly benefit from the canal.

Tourists have flocked to the canal since early phases of construction began. Intrigued by the great marvel of engineering, travelers came from all over the world. Many remarked on the comforts Americans had installed despite the rough, swampy surroundings. And tourism as an industry has only grown in Panama, especially as Panama has gained full control of the canal and improved efficiency and government stability. With the rise of **ecotourism**, tourism directed at endangered natural animals and locations, Panama has gained popularity for its rainforests, beaches, and biodiversity.

Thanks to its impressive biodiversity and rainforests, Panama is considered one of the best bird-watching sites on Earth.

Because Panama is on the path of migratory birds—including the greatest known hawk migration in the world and more than three million birds migrating over Panama City—it is considered one of the best birdwatching sites on Earth. Panama's key location on the water makes for great snorkeling, with views of sea turtles and dolphins, or whale-watching.

coast to the other—and the timing couldn't have been more important. The announcement of the opening of the long-awaited canal was overshadowed by the start of the First World War.

The benefit of moving large troops quickly and safely was pitted against the realization that other nations, possibly enemies, could do the same. Legally, the canal must be equally available to all nations, without discrimination. Therefore, the United States faced the prospect of aiding enemy ships through the canal they, themselves operated and had paid to build. Increased security was installed around the canal itself, and plans to build a two-ocean navy began to form. It is estimated that over $10 million (in 1925 currency) were spent annually to defend the canal.

In order to ensure against threats coming through the isthmus, in 1922 Congress ratified the Five-Power Treaty. As part of the treaty, naval limitations were negotiated between the United States, United Kingdom, France, Italy, and Japan. The treaty saved the United States significant naval spending until Japan pulled out in 1934.

As the military usefulness of the canal decreased after World War II, American officials began to question the value of keeping it. Just two years after World War II ended, President Harry Truman said, "Why don't we get out of Panama gracefully, before we are kicked out?" But it would be another thirty years before President Jimmy Carter returned the canal to Panama. And it would be more than twenty-two years after that before Panama would operate their own canal.

Chapter 4

The Major Players

In the 1500s, King Charles V of Spain was the first to attempt a trade route across the isthmus. For centuries after, leaders all over the world sought to build a canal across that narrow land-bridge. Yet it took hundreds of years before the technology was far enough advanced, and the need was strong enough to make it a reality. This special combination of circumstances came to pass at the end of the Industrial Revolution. By then, machines had more power, there was a greater world need to distribute goods, and there were more strategic military routes.

It took some of the most famous leaders and engineers of our time to build the long-awaited canal.

Opposite: *In 1977, President Carter and Panamanian dictator Omar Torrijos Herrera signed the Canal Treaty.*

Count Ferdinand de Lesseps

Ferdinand de Lesseps was born in 1805 in France. He took to politics at a young age, growing up in Italy where his father worked at the consulate. After college, he himself became assistant **vice-consul**, or assistant to other foreign officials, in Lisbon, Portugal, where his uncle was a diplomat. He moved to Tunis, in Tunisia, to work as vice-consul alongside his father. While in Africa, de Lesseps had many opportunities to prove himself politically as well as militarily because he was trusted on important missions in a volatile area.

In 1832, de Lesseps was sent to work in Alexandria, Egypt. There his ship was put in quarantine for a cholera epidemic. The head of the French Consulate in Alexandria sent him books while he waited on the ship. One book changed the trajectory of his life forever: Napoleon Bonaparte's plans for a Suez Canal.

The young, energetic vice-consul worked tirelessly in Egypt. He befriended local government officials and often traveled between Cairo and Alexandria to offer assistance during times of plague. During this time, over a third of the population of those cities died, and de Lesseps was no stranger to adversity and disease. This training would prove useful on the Panama Canal—but his experience wouldn't stop the huge labor losses on the canal project.

De Lesseps continued to travel Europe and North Africa, including a trip to Rome in 1849 to negotiate the peaceful return of the pope, Pius IX, to the Vatican. Changing politics and the elections in France put a halt to his work in Rome, however, and he was sent back to France. Only a few years later, in 1853, his wife and

Ferdinand Marie de Lesseps was made famous for his work on the Suez Canal but was unprepared for the challenges of the Central American climate and terrain.

one of his sons died within a few days of each other. De Lesseps found a distraction in Napoleon's plans for a canal through Egypt.

His foray into canal building was, perhaps, an odd one given de Lesseps's background. Because he was not an engineer himself, he relied on the knowledge of the best French engineers and his own enthusiasm and charisma to convince investors to take on the Suez Canal. Despite the many naysayers who criticized his plans, de Lesseps was able to build the canal. Not unlike the Panama Canal, James Burns writes in *Transforming Leadership*, "What actually built the canal—or excavated the first few tens of millions of cubic feet—was the forced labor of twenty thousand **fellahin** (peasants) supplied by the Egyptian government … [but] intensive mechanization gradually reduced the need for human labor."

Pleased with the results of the Suez Canal, de Lesseps insisted on a similar sea-level canal on his second massive undertaking, the Panama Canal. But this plan ignored the hilly geography, torrential rains, and mudslides that were never a problem in Egypt's flat, arid desert. His success in Egypt, however, had won him the trust of investors. Work on the new sea-level canal began in 1880 with enthusiasm.

The new project was a minefield of new problems ranging from the plans themselves to the difficult terrain and rampant disease. Frustrated with the project's slow progress and shrinking bank account, de Lesseps hired Gustav Eiffel to solve his problems. (Eiffel is the famous engineer who designed the Eiffel tower for the 1889 World's Fair in Paris, as well as the Statue of Liberty in New York City.) Joining the project after years of failures and frustrations, Eiffel began to plan a system of locks that might save the failing endeavor. Despite Eiffel's careful approach to the poorly managed project, Ferdinand de Lesseps's company collapsed. De Lesseps, de Lesseps's son Charles, and Gustav Eiffel were found guilty of fraud and maladministration. Eiffel was not himself responsible for the fraud, and his conviction was later reversed.

De Lesseps's long commitment to a sea-level canal hurt the project. So did his hesitation to listen to Dr. Carlos Finlay—the doctor who linked the spread of tropical diseases to mosquitos. In the end, excavation lasted nine years, resulted in the loss of at least seventeen thousand laborers, and ruined the fortunes of eight hundred thousand private investors. Some of these investors came from lower or middle classes and had hoped to improve their own way of life in France.

De Lesseps died just two years after his company went under, at the age of 89.

Dr. Carlos Finlay

Dr. Carlos Finlay was born in 1833 in Cuba. His father was a physician who had fought for independence from Spain alongside the revolutionary Simón Bolívar. Finlay pursued his early education in France and England. However, his European credentials would not be recognized back home in Havana. Once again, the young student left Cuba for school. This time he went to Jefferson Medical College in Philadelphia, Pennsylvania.

Much of Dr. Finlay's work was performed throughout the mid and late 1800s. Yet it wasn't until 1900 that the significance of his findings came to light. His first claim that mosquitos were responsible for the spread of disease—specifically yellow fever—

was made in 1881. His finding was well received at the 1881 International Sanitary Conference. Recommendations to eradicate mosquito populations followed. Sadly, it took twenty years for his advice to take hold. The inaction of de Lesseps in addressing the booming mosquito populations cost many laborers their lives.

It was Dr. Finlay's revolutionary finding that paved the way for Dr. William Gorgas's success in reducing yellow fever and malaria in the Panama Canal Zone during the American excavation. This medical breakthrough also helped improved health care and disease management all over the world.

President Theodore Roosevelt

President Theodore Roosevelt became the youngest president in America's history, entering office at the age of forty-two.

When President William McKinley was assassinated, Roosevelt—as the Republican vice president—was launched into a demanding job in a grieving nation. McKinley had been a man of the people and had supported economic growth. Other vice presidents who had assumed presidency under similar circumstances had not fared well in their new role as president. Roosevelt's role as vice president itself was the result of a political rival in New York (where Roosevelt was governor) nominating Roosevelt in order to keep Roosevelt out of the way of his own political ambitions. It must have been to that rival's dismay when Roosevelt assumed the presidency. But the new president took to the job with a vigor that even some of his fellow government officials were wary of.

President Theodore Roosevelt advocated for an active lifestyle and conservation of national land, such as Yosemite National Park in California.

Growing up as a sickly child, Roosevelt overcame his poor health and spent the rest of his life advocating the "strenuous life." He became a hunter, outdoorsman, and lover of nature. Though he grew up in New York, he moved to Montana to herd cattle. He joined the Rough Riders in the Spanish American War and became a hero. As president, he set aside land for national parks, recreation areas, and national forests.

It is no surprise that Roosevelt's adventurous spirit also led him to be the first president to venture outside the country while in office. Articles had started to condemn the canal project's poor working conditions and to accuse the government of having nefarious motivations, so the president went to see the construction of the canal himself. This visit was part of a huge public relations plan to win popular opinion in favor of the canal, which he boasted would benefit the entire world. His plan worked.

Roosevelt was reelected for a second term and served as president from 1901 to 1908. The Panama Canal was one of the Roosevelt administration's pet projects, and the president took an active role in the organization, leadership, and labor disputes that arose. Concerns over segregation, wages, work hours, and sanitation all filtered up to the president through the engineers he placed in command of the building effort.

Roosevelt ended his presidency in 1909 after promising not to run for a third term. Even so, he practically hand-picked his successor, William Howard Taft, and helped the reluctant politician get elected. But by the end of a four-year term, Taft had alienated his own party. Roosevelt ran again in a new political party named after himself—the Bull Moose Party. Though he gained support, he split the Republican voters. Roosevelt lost the election to Woodrow Wilson.

The completion of the canal—the crowning jewel of Roosevelt's presidency—was announced in 1914 with little fanfare. Preoccupied by the First World War, the greatest marvel of human engineering went quietly unnoticed.

The Bull Moose president passed away in January of 1919. Though he'd been ill, his doctors were still surprised. Roosevelt had seemed unstoppable.

A String of Engineers

John Wallace

Upon beginning excavation of the canal, chief engineer John Wallace found himself immediately overwhelmed. French equipment had been left in disrepair or abandoned to rust. The tropical diseases that tormented the French excavation teams were no less threatening to the American labor force. Wallace also faced a wall of bureaucracy in the canal commission back in Washington, DC. Despite being the highest paid government employee under Roosevelt (at $25,000 a year), all of his decisions on the isthmus had to be approved by the committee in the far-away capital.

Frustrated with the mountains of work and feeling powerless to take action himself, Wallace quit after only one year in Panama.

John Stevens

In 1905, John Stevens, who had formerly worked on railroads in the Unites States, took over the position as chief engineer. Stevens fared a bit better, tackling labor issues by bringing in West Indian workers and replacing dilapidated equipment. It was also Stevens who pushed for better sanitation to keep workers healthy. He brought on Dr. William Gorgas, who knew the mosquitos had to be eliminated to stop the outbreaks of yellow fever and malaria. Stevens noted the dangerous mudslides that buried men and machines alike. He pushed for a new, better engineering plan in response. He suggested building the canal as a series of locks rather than a sea-level canal. This saved the United States the same disastrous outcome as the French. Under Stevens's supervision, the canal excavation began in earnest. The new equipment began shoveling tons of earth away daily, filling trains that carted the dirt and debris to Lake Gatun, where it would form the dam.

Despite his massive contribution to the effort of building the canal, by 1907 Stevens was also weary. He had done constant battle with the committee in Washington who did not always grasp the needs of the people in the isthmus. He resigned in February of that year.

Colonel George Washington Goethals

Roosevelt appointed an army engineer, Colonel George Washington Goethals, to replace Stevens on the project. The president believed Goethals would run the construction site like the military—with order and hierarchy. To ensure he wouldn't lose yet another chief engineer, Roosevelt dismantled the canal commission that had made leadership in the isthmus so difficult in the past. In doing so, he granted Goethals the utmost authority in the Canal Zone.

Goethals didn't disappoint. If a mudslide undid part of the excavation, he would coolly demand it be re-dug. He ran a tight ship, insisting that segregation and pay rates linked to race would help maintain efficiency. He would listen to any complaints or feedback anyone in the Canal Zone had—ranging from the washer women in the laundry, to the train operators—but only on Sundays. Rarely did anything come of the complaints, and Goethals wouldn't let workers take matters into their own hands. He encouraged the Zone police to spy

George W. Goethals brought his military training to the job. His strict rules were partly responsible for the efficiency of the project's completion.

on workers and their meetings in order to catch people who stayed home from work, to squash attempted **strikes**, and to break apart the formation of **unions**. When workers saw their complaints going unanswered, they reached out to unions in the United States who might represent them to higher courts outside the Zone. Goethals often accused the laborers of being spoiled and lazy. He believed they were asking for too much.

Poultney Bigelow

A journalist and outspoken opponent of the Panama Canal Project, Poultney Bigelow may have presented the greatest obstacle to Roosevelt's effort to win favor with the public. Many journalists traveled to Panama to write about the engineering marvel and impressive American comforts brought to such a difficult tropical climate. Bigelow, however, interviewed impoverished workers living in unsanitary conditions.

In 1906, Bigelow wrote in the *New York Times*, "Colón to-day is mainly a swamp, into which is dumped all the human excrement of the negro population and where this population is compelled to sleep. There is no water at Colón save this swamp water and what can be collected by the dripping from the roofs of the shanties. The sanitary inspection at Colón is a sham."

It was these harsh criticisms of the canal's labor conditions that propelled President Roosevelt away from Washington, DC, and into the heart of the isthmus. Roosevelt was determined to show the American public (the tax payers who were funding the project) that things weren't so bad there. His trip suggested conditions were fit for a president.

Despite his lack of sympathy for the workers, he was respected, if not admired, for his strong sense of organization and productivity. Visiting engineers and the press were in awe of what he'd managed to accomplish, especially in light of the difficulties France and previous engineers had faced. Today, we see that Goethal's legacy is tainted by his racist attitudes and the way he treated his workers.

Omar Torrijos

Omar Torrijos was never elected president of Panama. Instead, he took over the government in a *coup d'état* and held a variety of titles, like "Maximum Leader of the Panamanian Revolution" and "Supreme Chief of Government." But Torrijos's rise to power does not mean he was a bad leader or that he was unloved by the citizens of his country.

Torrijos's reign lasted from 1968 to 1981. It was marked by a number of progressive and social reforms intended to improve the lives of the Panamanian citizens. These included opening schools and creating jobs.

In 1977, Torrijos negotiated with President Jimmy Carter for the United States to hand over control of the Panama Canal to Panama. The United States was seeing fewer benefits from the canal. It was expensive to maintain and operate—especially with the additional cost of paying large sums to the Panamanian government.

Ovidio Diaz-Espino told PBS in an interview:

> Panamanians felt they were not benefitting from the canal. And there was a fence. As

General Omar Torrijos negotiated the peaceful transfer of the Panama Canal from the United States to Panama.

> a child growing up, I could not go into the Canal Zone because I was Panamanian. It was pure American land. This was the most valuable piece of land in the country, and it was being exploited by somebody else. There was a lot of conflict leading to massacres, students killed by soldiers because they tried to raise a Panamanian flag at the Canal. It was an unstable situation.

The populist Panamanian leader had earned the trust of American leaders, and the treaty he negotiated allowed the United States to intervene if the security of the canal was ever threatened. In fact, it was the watchful eye of America's military that allowed Panama to take over the canal without threat from neighboring countries. The treaty also encouraged the new Panamanian leadership to avoid corruption by keeping the canal entirely separate from the Panamanian government.

The respected leader died in a plane crash at the age of fifty-two. The Panama Canal expansion was to go on without Torrijo, though. It was completed in the summer of 2016.

IN MEMORY OF

Chapter 5

The Effects of the Panama Canal

On his 1913 visit to Washington, the ambassador from Panama shared his excitement for the canal, "Our country has the canal within its own territory, and therefore enjoys the greatest advantage." Yet one of the remarkable results of the Panama Canal's construction is how little direct influence it had on Panama. However, since the canal has been returned to its home country, it's easier to see the ways Panama might have been affected if they'd been able to be more involved.

For Better or Worse

While many trade routes are significant for bringing multiple cultures in contact with one another, the Panama Canal rarely played that role. Perhaps one of the most interesting aspects of the canal is how **insulated** Panama itself was from the canal for so long.

Opposite: *The United States flag flies alongside the Panamanian flag in the Canal Zone.*

The United States made expansion a central focus of the American legacy. First, Westward expansion took place and came at significant cost to Native Americans across the continental United States. Later, in the nineteenth century, the United States began aiding other nations—like Cuba, Puerto Rico, Guam, Philippines, and Hawaii—in their fight for independence from European powers. Then Americans seized the benefits from the fledgling nations for themselves. The construction of the Panama Canal is an example of American imperialism. While the canal cut through Panama, Panamanians reaped little benefit from its existence until much later.

Even so, there are a few ways that the Panama Canal changed its home country. The primary effect was that Panama became a country at all. Panama was aided in their liberation movement and was able to become an independent nation precisely because the United States wanted to build the canal.

Orlando Perez, author of *Political Culture in Panama*, told PBS:

> For Panamanian nationals at the time, this was the accomplishment of their dreams, to position Panama at the heart of a global commercial enterprise or system, to use the geographic location of Panama to its commercial advantage. Geography has always determined Panamanian politics and the economy. The problem was how that accomplishment came about ... The payment [to Panamanians] was substantial, but it wasn't anywhere near the benefits that the US would

> accrue. So the Panamanians started with the great hope that it would place Panama at the center of world commerce, but also resenting that they achieved this victory at the cost of ceding sovereignty over the Canal itself.

During the construction of the canal, the United States deliberately hired cheaper foreign labor, rather than provide jobs to their new host and protectorate. The government also demanded that canal employees be exempt from paying taxes to Panama. Furthermore, it forbade local businesses from providing goods and services in the Canal Zone or to ships passing through. This was not entirely abusive—at least not intentionally. When workers first arrived in the Zone, local food production was overwhelmed. Businesses took advantage of foreign workers who had no other options.

For example, a worker might be expected to pay a full day's wages for a single egg. With nowhere else to buy food, he or she would have to pay the unreasonable fee. Due to poor sanitation, the safety of the food was also called into question.

In response, the canal "Commissary" was instituted. It maintained fair prices for goods, most of them imported from the United States. Even livestock was brought in from other South American countries and raised in the Zone. This was because fear of "cattle fever" and other diseases in local cattle scared workers off. These measures, though they appeared necessary at the time, cut Panama out of the canal project altogether. Even after Panama addressed many of the original concerns, the United States still banned "importing" meats and dairy from Panama.

Public Health

One of the greatest accomplishments of the canal project was discovering the link between mosquitos and tropical infectious diseases like malaria. The United States's motivation was selfish—to keep their own workers alive so they could keep working. Yet the discovery was not without benefits to the people of Panama.

American hospitals, like this one in Ancon, dotted the Canal Zone. Hospitals provided employment for many American women who came to Panama in search of jobs and adventure.

The Harvard Business School reports that malarial death rates fell from 2 percent to .2 percent between 1906 and 1909. In the largest Panamanian cities, Panama City and Colón, the decline of malaria accounted for 37 to 40 percent of the decline in the mortality rate.

Gorgas's methods were thorough, if a little extreme. To prepare for canal workers, sanitation officials traveled throughout the 50 miles (80.5 km) of the Canal Zone to fumigate buildings, drain standing water (or pour oil or poison in the water instead), construct sewers and waterlines, poison thousands of rats, and even kill hundreds of stray dogs who could act as **hosts** for mosquitos. During the project, the sanitation department used 700,000 gallons (2.65 million liters) of oil and 124,000 gallons (469,391 liters) of insecticide *every year*.

Vector-borne diseases (illnesses spread from one organism to another by feeding) were still poorly understood. In addition to rampant malaria and yellow fever, the canal workers also faced an outbreak of the plague (the same disease that killed twenty-five million Europeans in the fourteenth century).

Though the Panamanian people were well insulated from the Canal Zone and its cultural or economic benefits, it seems the greatest immediate contribution the Panama Canal made in its home country was the decline of disease.

The author of *The Canal Builders*, Julie Greene, says, "The US wanted to frame a vision of itself as more selfless [and] advancing civilization. Of course there's the other side to that: often the US was, despite its self-image, imposing its power. In Panama, it asserted its power over the republic and dominated the county's history for 100 years."

This is not to say there haven't been important and lasting benefits to Panama—in addition to liberation from Colombia, the canal brought new methods of sanitation that drastically reduced malaria and yellow fever. Eventually, the canal was returned to Panama. And the nation has found a way to make the canal more lucrative for their own country than it was for the United States.

Economics

A British visitor to the Canal Zone once commented on America's spending—noting that the club houses, ice boxes, and entertainments were a uniquely American touch in the face of the task at hand. Luxury aside, the canal itself came at an astronomical cost. Some economists estimate the canal cost at as much as 921.7 million 1925 dollars, roughly equivalent to 119.4 *billion* dollars today. As a result, economists have asked, reasonably, *Was it worth it?*

Given the massive expense, both in money and lives, was the canal a good investment for the United States? After compiling an exhaustive report, the Harvard Business School decided it was. They report:

> The Panama Canal is one of the first great works of twentieth century engineering.

> It dramatically cut transportation costs and produced significant savings for world commerce. The lion's share of these savings were captured by the United States, because most of the ships passing through the Canal carried cargoes coming from or destined to the United States—or in the case of the intercoastal traffic, both—and because the Canal produced significant direct transfers to the U.S. Treasury. Despite the large cost overruns during its construction, and the prolonged construction time, the Canal was a good investment of public money.

Instant Gratification

Transportation and shipping costs dropped by 20 to 30 percent after the opening of the canal. These benefits were especially felt in the United States, which had ports on either side of the canal. Europe and Asia had other routes for trading with one another, such as the Suez Canal and traveling around the horn of Africa. Therefore, they used the canal only when trading with the United States. In fact, 75 percent of the canal's traffic had its origins or terminus in the United States, and 40 percent of that was made up of American vessels traveling from one coast to the other.

The immediate improvement in transportation was enormous at the time. The time it takes to cross the canal is eight to ten hours, versus weeks traveling around all of South America. Between thirteen thousand and fourteen thousand ships use the canal every year, many of which are American. The next most frequent users are China, Chile, Japan, Colombia, and South Korea. Tolls for the canal are calculated by a ship's size and cargo volume. The largest ships can spend as much as $450,000 in **tariffs** to use the canal. (Remember that the United States's original contract with Panama stipulated they pay only $250,000 total each year.) In 1928, Richard Halliburton, an American adventurer, swam through the canal and paid 36 cents. This was the smallest toll ever paid in the canal.

For a short time, especially during the election of 1912 between Taft, Roosevelt, and Wilson, the American public and government pushed for free tolls for domestic American ships passing through the canal. This was an important issue on the campaign trail for the candidates because citizens saw the use of the canal as a right. Americans thought free passage should be given in return for having spent so much to build it. Additionally, tolls affect shipping costs, which affect a business's operating costs. These factors ultimately set the price of goods for consumers. This push for no-toll travel for American ships was called the Panama Canal Act. It passed by a landslide in the Senate.

Woodrow Wilson ran for president in 1912 in favor of eliminating tolls for American ships. After being elected president, however, he was informed this was impossible. To do so would be in violation of the Hay-Pauncefont Treaty, which said the United States would be allowed to manage the canal only as long as all nations were able to use the canal without discrimination. Wilson was advised that the British were angry about the idea of paying tolls when Americans didn't have to. The British, therefore, might not renew their own Arbitration Convention agreement with the United States. The Arbitration Agreement said that disagreements between the two countries would be settled by an independent arbitrator who was not a part of their own government. Worried about international relations, as well as what subsidies other American transport companies would demand, Wilson was able to repeal the Panama Canal Act.

The economic advantage of the canal reached its peak in 1930. That's when it had saved governments and businesses around the world $1.5 billion in total. Gradually, though, the canal became obsolete in the United States. In the wake of World War II, the United States worried that canal access put them at greater military risk than it provided an advantage. Additionally, the rail system proved a more effective way to ship soldiers from home to ports on either side of the country. Years later, highway systems, commercial flight, and other methods made transporting goods faster and cheaper. As early as 1939, there had been talk of expanding the canal to meet the demands of growing ships. After spending $72.5 million over the course of a few years, however, the expansion was canceled.

The Cost of Dissent

In 1959, Jose Antonio Remon, Panama's president, was assassinated. After decades of American control over Panama and its canal and the loss of their own leader, riots and protests broke out among citizens. For weeks, American businesses in Panama were the targets of looting and violence. In response, President Eisenhower authorized the Panamanian flag to fly alongside the United States's flag in the Canal Zone. He also required more Panamanian goods be purchased by the Zone. The United States increased their aid to the Panamanian government to stop the unrest. As

America spent more on Panama, keeping the canal became increasingly expensive.

In 1977, President Jimmy Carter signed a treaty that would return the canal to Panama at the turn of the century. In 1999, Panama finally began operating the Panama Canal.

Author Orlando Perez told PBS:

> The Panamanians have done a marvelous job at running it. It's efficient and profitable. It's run independent of the Panamanian government. There have been very few reported or alleged cases of corruption within management. It's a very efficient, moneymaking enterprise, and I think everyone that looks at how Panamanians have handled the management, creating an authority for it, they wish the national government was run as efficiently and effectively as that.

Recently, adding larger locks that can accommodate some of the world's largest ships cost roughly $5.25 billion. Still, with increased traffic that is charged by its cargo, the expansion is expected to be worth the investment.

Managing a World Wonder

So how was Panama able to extract greater value from the canal than the United States?

As they had done during the construction of the canal, the United States had employed expensive American workers for the highest paying jobs, and cheaper (finally local) labor for unskilled positions.

This naturally spread tensions between the Canal Zone and Panama, but it also encouraged inefficiency. Maurer and Yo report, "The chief executives of the Panama Canal Company … were neither drawn from private industry, nor ambitious younger members of the civil service, nor political appointees anxious to perform well. Rather, they were military bureaucrats at the end of their careers, given a plum job as a reward before retirement."

Without incentives to perform better, or make the canal more lucrative, the canal floundered. In an attempt to save money, the Canal Company cut roughly five thousand employees, nearly 30 percent of the staff. These were, however, low-wage workers. Further attempts were made to tighten the Canal Company's finances. These included reducing the **differential**, or difference in American and Panamanian pay given to American employees, and denying the differential be paid to married women at all. These choices were often at the expense of the average worker.

As budgets were decreased, worker dissatisfaction increased, and so did accidents and their degree of seriousness (and how expensive the accidents were to fix). As costs and opposition mounted, multiple presidents looked for a way out of the Canal Zone. The American public, however, saw the canal as a symbol of American success. They worried that returning it to Panama would suggest weakness in their own nation.

When Panama took control of the canal, the situation did not improve overnight. In the 1980s, shipping declined and Panama's government underwent an administration change that negatively affected business. A Panamanian politician and military leader, Manuel Noriega, was using the government and

In the 1980s, Manuel Noriega, a corrupt politician, took control of Panama.

its affiliation with the United States to make money in drug running and money laundering. The offense that finally led the United States to remove Noriega from power, though, was when he killed Panama's former minister of health, and forced the president he had helped elect (likely falsely) to resign. When United States officials disapproved of these actions, Noriega threatened American military personnel and Panamanian employees of the canal. Noriega was replaced by Guillermo Endara.

The treaties between the United States and Panama included a twenty-year transfer period of the canal between governments. Thanks in part to the long transition period and its coincidental alignment with a new, popularly elected leader (Endara), Panama's workforce was well-trained and the canal itself was protected from the previous government's corruption. It thrived.

After Noriega was removed from government, the new canal staff deliberately separated canal operations from the government so jobs would not be offered in exchange for political favors. The ports at Colón and Panama City were privatized to further avoid any government interference. In order to make the canal profitable again, the new canal leadership raised tolls and looked for ways to cut costs. More than 30 percent of the work force was cut, saving $40 million—but this time it was largely high paid American workers who voluntarily retired. Profits rose from 5 percent to 20 percent. Higher profits allowed the new administration to reinvest in the canal, making repairs and improving safety. As a result, fewer accidents occurred, saving additional money.

Innovations in management of the canal also improved efficiency and safety. Management ended the practice of two-way traffic in the canal, designating half the day for traffic traveling from the Atlantic to the Pacific, and half the day for Pacific-to-Atlantic traffic. They also added incentives. For instance, ships could pay for a reservation, which allowed them to skip to the front of the line if they arrived on time. By 2006, nearly 60 percent of canal traffic requested a reservation. By 2008, the canal was generating $701 million in revenue for the Republic of Panama.

The Environment

Abdiel Perez, the superintendent of the locks on the Atlantic side of the canal, says, "The Panama Canal is like a wound humans inflicted on the Earth … that nature is trying to heal." For all its engineering and economic glory—why would the canal's own superintendent hold such a belief?

Maintenance

In his book, *The World Without Us*, Alan Weisman makes it clear that, although the canal opened in 1914 and became fully operational in 1920, the work there will never be done. In fact, workers are still *digging* the canal. Because Lake Gatun is in the path of a river, tons of silt is carried into the lake that needs to be constantly removed to keep the waterway clear for ships. In 1935, an additional dam had to be built upriver from Lake Gatun to control the massive flood waters that poured into the lake and risked **capsizing** ships. This additional dam, known as Madden Dam, also needs constant attention. Workers continue to clear away jungle plants from both areas because the root systems of these plants threaten to break apart the walls of the dams. Workers also watch for natural springs that come up through the ground and the walls of the dams.

The rims of the dam are made with earth excavated from digging the canal and lake. This compacted earth can erode away or quickly become grown over. One canal worker told Weisman that he came to work one day looking for part of the dam and couldn't find it because "nature had eaten it." Without humans there to control nature, Weisman suggests, the canal could be swallowed by the earth in a single rainy season.

Long Term Effects

But there have been other, more direct environmental effects of the canal construction. Clearing the way for the canal's excavation required roughly 30,000,000 pounds (13,607,771.1 kg) of explosives that obliterated roughly 50 miles (80.5 km) of wildlife habitats, as well as a few native villages. When Lake Gatun was originally filled, it drowned an entire mahogany forest. It took six thousand men digging every day for seven years to dig the lake alone. This process also took the homes of many native species along with the dirt. The loss of of the trees themselves is only part of the concern. The rains from dense, tropical rainforests provide Panama with drinking water, **irrigation** water, and fill the canal with the 52,000 gallons (196,841.4 liters) of freshwater needed to lift boats from one ocean to the other. Much of the canal water is eventually dumped in the ocean when ships come out the other side and won't be used again.

These forests are also home to native wildlife that cannot survive in other habitats, as well as migratory birds who depend on the trees for shelter as they travel from one continent to the next every season. This loss of biodiversity has an economic impact. Panama benefits from roughly two million tourists who visit every year and pump money into the economy. In addition to being drawn to the famous Panama Canal, tourists also come to see the rainforest and exotic animals. Ecotourism is a booming industry in Panama.

For many years, Lake Gatun was the largest manmade lake on Earth.

And it could be lost with the loss of its vast rainforests.

Luckily, Panama began the expansion project on the new set of locks with a reforestation initiative. In order to stop the rapid rate of deforestation—roughly 195,000 acres (78,913.7 ha) of trees are lost a year—Panama has started to encourage private investors to buy land and replant the trees. A new law, Law 24, gives investors taxes cuts and residency eligibility. This might draw investors from all over the world.

Panama's official forestry website notes that by investing $80,000 in a reforestation project, foreigners are eligible to apply for a visa. The investment can be attractive for people hoping to retire in Panama or relocate for other reasons. Many foreign investors may come from other South and Central American countries. They could be drawn to Panama for its job opportunities and relative stability.

Chapter 6

The Future of the Canal

The Panama Canal has had a long and winding history. It has involved political maneuvering and mixed economic success. The building of the canal especially was fraught with setbacks and ethical dilemmas. The recent expansion, it turns out, is no different.

The Expansion

As with any complex issue or historical event, there will always been benefits and drawbacks. America's amazing feat of engineering, for example, came at an enormous cost to poor workers, the environment, American taxpayers, and to Panama itself. Yet some of the decisions the United States made when they blocked the sale of Panamanian food and goods were to protect their labors. The burden of the cost of building the canal fell on American citizens.

Opposite: *The Panama Canal's expansion in 2016 allows ships to pass carrying nearly three times as much cargo as the original merchant ships that traveled through the canal.*

Yet those same citizens enjoyed the reduced cost of goods, and businesses were able to sell their wares internationally and thrive in a growing global market.

These same tradeoffs exist today. As Panama sees increased gains from the canal and expands to keep this famous trade route relevant, costs and labor disputes once again become issues of the enormous building project. But the hope that the larger canal will lead to economic gains still lingers on the horizon.

The Expansion at Work

The recent canal expansion took ten years and $5.25 billion to complete. Compare this with the combined original French and American construction, which took nineteen years and cost the US alone $119 billion (in today's dollars). The expansion will allow larger ships, called **Neo-Panamax** ships, to pass through the Panama Canal. This new capability will help it take on new business and higher tariffs. On the verge of becoming obsolete in the face of new technologies, the canal had to get an update to provide its basic services to the growing ships that transport goods around the world.

Today, just as in the early 1900s, canal workers are still concerned with fair wages and safe working conditions. Though it was finally completed, the new canal expansion project was delayed more than two years by labor stoppages and issues with funding.

In 2015, for example, a union-led strike of six thousand laborers threatened to further delay progress on the expansion. It was avoided only after the builders met the workers' demands for higher pay.

Opposite: *With almost no room for error in the new, expanded locks, canal workers who pull the massive ships through the canal worry the expansion won't be safe.*

Wide receiver

Panama wants to attract new ships from Asia that carry significantly more cargo – requiring a deeper and wider canal – and help the vessels get to East Coast harbors.

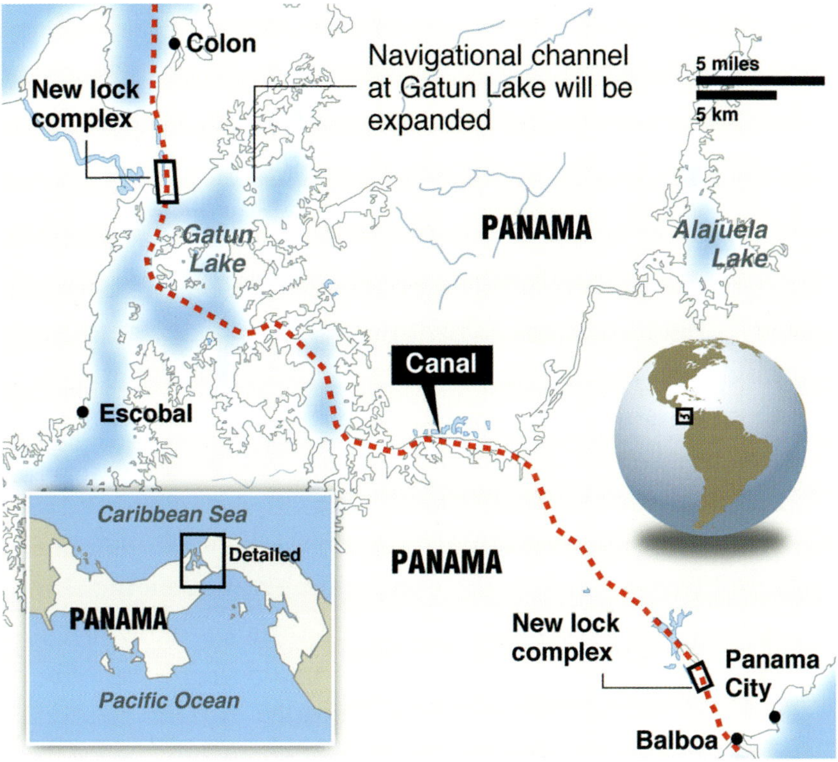

Comparing old and new canal locks

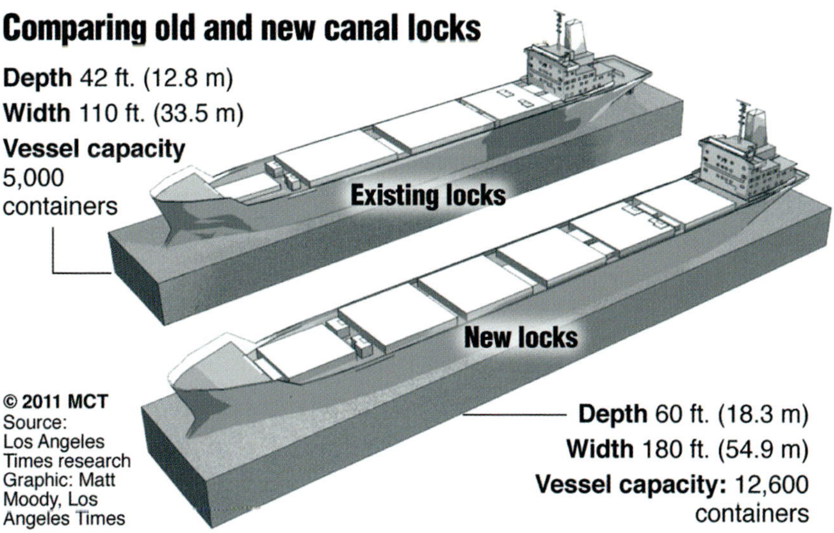

Source: Los Angeles Times research
Graphic: Matt Moody, Los Angeles Times

Workers saw a 9 percent increase in pay as a result. Today, workers have continued to advocate for their own rights and wages, just as workers on the original canal would petition Goethals. A key difference, however, is the existence of unions, which have greater power than individuals.

Though workers are treated much better today than they were in Roosevelt's time, the expansion has faced its fair share of obstacles. The Spanish company that won the bid to build the new expansion proposed such a low cost to build—only $3 billion—that going over budget was seen as inevitable. Perhaps even more problematic was the effort to cut costs to stay within the unrealistic budget, which was a billion dollars lower than the next lowest proposed bid. To reduce costs, the cement used to build the canal was not of high quality. It was supposed to last 100 years but started leaking before the expansion even opened. The company that insured the new project was also skeptical of the small budget for concrete—71 percent less than that of the next lowest bidder. Another issue is the size of the new, larger locks themselves. They were built with little extra space around the new, enormous ships. Some have hit the walls, causing expensive damage to the boats and the locks.

The original locks have long used trains to guide ships through the canal. Strong cables connect ships to trains on either side of the canal, holding the vessels in place so they won't hit the concrete sides of the canal. Looking for a less expensive method, the new expansion implemented the use of tugboats. The tugboat operators have repeatedly had issues with the new fleet of boats. With so little room for error between the ships and the walls of the locks, the tugboats have to be perfectly controlled. Yet tugboat captains have called the boats "perfectly awful." They report that the boats are difficult to maneuver. In fact, they seem to work better going *backwards*. This is impossible while pulling some of the largest ships on the ocean into the tight locks. The new tugboats are a challenge to maneuver even under perfect conditions, but those conditions are rare. In the event of strong winds or choppy water, this delicate and precise job becomes nearly hopeless. Being stuck between a lock and a hard place (or massive cargo ship, as the case may be) is incredibly dangerous for the tugboat captains. They worry their boats could be crushed with the slightest error.

Engineers foresaw many of these issues before building began. But just as de Lesseps stuck to his sea-level plan until it was too late, the canal administration stuck with their original plan for the new expansion. The new locks have been open since June of 2016. More time is needed tell if the reinforced walls will last 100 years as promised and if the fleet of tugboats will be able to do their job safely.

Safety aside, the tugboats themselves are a point of contention. Despite Panama's plan not to pay favors by granting canal jobs, the *New York Times* found documents that showed "the canal authority bought the tugboats for $158 million from a company later represented by the son of Jorge L. Quijano, the canal's administrator."

Even with these setbacks and problems, Panama remains hopeful about the benefits of the expansion. They hope to increase the canal's contribution to their **Gross Domestic Product (GDP)**, or the value of goods and services they produce, from 5 percent to 40 percent.

The Shipping Yard

The expansion of the Panama Canal doesn't just affect Panama. The expansion means larger ships will be reaching ports across the eastern coast of the United States. This will cause ports in Baltimore, Charleston, Miami, New York, and Savannah to take on their own expansion projects to accommodate the giant new ships. *The Economist* reported that, "The Port Authority of New York and New Jersey plans to spend $2.7 billion on enlarging its terminals and shipping lanes, and a further $1.3 billion to raise a bridge by 20 metres."

The Neo-Panamax ships are expected to carry fourteen thousand 20-foot (6.1 m) containers each. This capacity is nearly three times the load of ships passing through the original canal. The Associated Press reports that "Some 35 to 40 vessels transit the waterway each day, and the canal is estimated to handle about 6 percent of world maritime commerce." Of course, more ships mean more money for Panama.

According to the *New York Times*, "Shippers will pay an estimated $800,000 to send a neo-Panamax vessel through the canal." However, the newspaper also says this about the recent setbacks stemming from the new canal's design: "dents and delays are not good for business."

It seems also that the canal may never be big enough to keep up with ship builders. While the expansion allows the canal to take on a new fleet of super-sized ships, it is already too small for the next class of larger ships. These include Maersk's Triple E class ships, which can carry eighteen thousand 20-foot (6.1 m) containers. These new ships—the largest container ships in the world—measure

The new Neo-Panamax ships can carry as many as fourteen thousand 20-foot (6 m) containers and will pay canal tariffs of nearly $800,000 per trip.

194 feet (59.1 m) wide and 1,312 feet (399.9 m) long. They suggest that another canal expansion may just be a hundred years away.

Trade and Commerce

The expansion was designed to accommodate increasing shipping traffic and the growing size of the loads ships can transport through the locks. Yet the expanded canal lanes opened during a lull in international shipping. China, the canal's new biggest customer, is experiencing an economic slowdown. This has resulted in fewer Chinese ships taking goods through the canal. As Panama prepared to open the expanded canal, a Chinese company purchased the largest port in Panama. This purchase has some people nervous, since the privately owned company is suspected of being controlled by the Chinese government. Therefore, Panama's biggest economic asset may once again be influenced by a foreign nation. A Chinese billionaire has also considered building a competing shipping route through Nicaragua. The project would fulfill the United States's initial vision for a South American canal. However, it could present devastating competition for Panama.

Even the United States seems to be competing with the canal. Worried about losing their shipping business with Asia to the East Coast, ports on the West Coast are making improvements to make shipping through them more attractive. *The Economist* reports, "Shipping a box from Shanghai to New York takes 26 days via Panama. Shipping it to California and completing the journey by train takes only 21 days (though it costs more). West-coast ports are modernising [sic] in a bid to 'beat the canal.'" Beyond appeal, these changes are due to bare necessity. Lower oil prices around the world have reduced the need to bring oil and fossil fuels through the canal. And fossil fuels are one of the primary goods that is transported with the new, large ships.

Across the world, the Suez Canal has lowered its tariffs by 65 percent to stay competitive and encourage shipping through its canal. Such a reduction in prices may encourage shipping companies to take longer routes through the Suez if it means saving money. For Panama, this may mean lowering their own tolls, even on the heels of the expensive new expansion.

Antonio Dominguez, a general manager for global shipping leader Maersk Line, says, "It's important to remember that the canal does not create demand. The canal opens the route. Supply and demand on a world

Expansion in Panama has meant expansion for many ports along America's East Coast.

level is what will decide whether the Panama Canal will really bring more volume or not."

As concerns for the canal are growing, so are concerns for the shipping industry as a whole. Fewer goods are sent around the world. Thus more ships sit idle or are underpaid for their cargo. As *Fortune Magazine* put it, "It's probably a better time to own a canal than a ship."

The Canal and You

The cost of shipping affects the cost of goods being shipped around the world. Decreased tariffs can mean lower costs for the goods you and your family purchase. It can also alter the delicate balance of supply and demand, as well as how many employees a company can hire if they make less money. In turn,

Water and the Canal

A concern to engineers and environmentalists alike are the **droughts**, or periods of unusually low rainfall, that Panama has recently faced. Droughts threaten the levels of Lake Gatun, which supports shipping—one of the most important industries for the small country's economy. Residents also depend on Lake Gatun as a reservoir for their clean, fresh water. The lake is so central to people's lives that when levels became dangerously low, the canal's administrator accused citizens of "using too much tap water."

The isthmus has historically been a very wet place. In fact, torrential rains got in the way of canal construction for anyone who attempted it. But now that the locks have been built, these same rains are needed to fill the locks of the canal and send boats through. The canal depends on 26,700,000 gallons (101,070,495 l) of water pouring down from Lake Gatun to move ships through the canal. If the locks are not filled adequately, or Lake Gatun isn't deep enough, boats can run aground, causing massive damage.

Even in the new canal's short life, the risk presented by low water levels has caused the canal administration to demand ships reduce their cargo so boats will be lighter and be able to pass safely through the locks. In some cases, a ship's cargo has been reduced to the amount traditionally shipped through the original canal, eliminating the benefit of the expanded canal.

The goods that line the shelves of stores all over the world are made available by the intricate web of international trade routes, like the Panama Canal.

these shifts affect jobs, wages, and the spending money available to the average citizen. Furthermore, there are consequences as technology improves and more goods become electronic. Take downloading a new album rather than buying a CD at the store, for intance. A CD would have been made by someone in a factory, shipped by someone who works for a distributor, and sold by a cashier. Therefore, many traditional industries must make big changes to survive.

All of these factors come together in ways you may not see directly. Yet they shape the global economy and indirectly affect your daily life. The Panama Canal may seem like a far-off shipping route from the old days, but its role in global trade ties its future to the lives of people all over the world.

Glossary

Bucyrus digger A large steam-powered shovel.

cadavers Dead bodies used to teach medical students anatomy.

capsizing The act of a boat flipping upside-down.

convoy A group of ships or vehicles, often accompanied by military protection.

differential The difference between two amounts.

drought Shortage or scarcity, usually of water.

ecotourism Tourism that focuses on rare and endangered animals and wildlife.

expatriates Foreigners living in a country, usually for the purpose of working there.

fellahin Egyptian peasants.

Gross Domestic Product (GDP) The total value of goods and services a country produces.

hosts A living organism used as food for a dependent organism.

immune Without risk.

imperialism Control of foreign governments and politics.

indigenous Native populations.

Industrial Revolution The period from roughly 1760 to 1830 when factories and machines began producing goods.

inflation Decreased value of currency (corresponding to increased cost of goods).

irrigation Water for crops.

isthmus A narrow land bridge.

locks Gated waterways.

maritime Commercial or military activity on the sea.

Neo-Panamax (New Panamax) The largest ship that can be transported through the new, expanded Panama Canal locks.

Panamax The largest ship that can be transported through the original Panama Canal.

perpetuity An arrangement that continues indefinitely.

strikes Organized refusals to work in order to demand higher wages or better working conditions.

tariffs Tolls.

union A group of laborers in a given field who work together to protect their rights.

vector-borne diseases Diseases passed from one contaminated species to another.

Further Information

Websites

American Experience: The Panama Canal
http://www.pbs.org/wgbh/americanexperience/films/panama/
Explore primary source documents, photo galleries, videos, and more on PBS's companion website to their documentary about the Panama Canal.

How the Panama Canal Works
http://waitbutwhy.com/2014/09/panama-canal-works.html
Watch a video of how locks are the foundation of the Panama Canal.

Theodore Roosevelt
https://www.whitehouse.gov/1600/presidents/theodoreroosevelt
Learn more about the twenty-sixth president and his role in the construction of the Panama Canal.

Books

Keller, Ulrich. *The Building of the Panama Canal in Historic Photographs*. New York: Dover Publications, 1984.

Lunde, Darrin. *The Naturalist: Theodore Roosevelt, A Lifetime of Exploration*. New York: Crown, 2016.

Paine, Lincoln. *The Sea & Civilization: A Maritime History of the World.* New York: Vintage, 2015.

Shah, Sonia. *The Fever: How Malaria Has Ruled Humankind for 5000 years*. New York: Picador, 2011.

Weisman, Alex. *The World Without Us*. New York: Thomas Dunn Books, 2007.

Videos

"How the Panama Canal Was Built"
https://www.youtube.com/watch?v=q2T7CL9wqyM
BBC News provides a short overview of the challenges that were overcome to build the canal.

"Steaming Across Panama: Bucyrus and the Digging of the Panama Canal"
http://www.youtube.com/watch?v=2S3w1h_Pd_8
With images illustrating the challenge of digging out the Panama Canal, this video gives the history of the Bucyrus digger and its important role in the excavation of the canal.

Bibliography

Barrett, John, and Pan American Union. *Panama Canal: What It Is, What It Means*. Washington, DC: Pan American Union, 1913.

Bigelow, Poultney. "Panama: Poultney Bigelow Reaffirms His Criticisms of the Canal Work." *New York Times,* January 12, 1906. http://query.nytimes.com/mem/archive-free/ pdf?res= 9D0OE4DD103EE733A2575 1C1A9679C946 797D6CF.

Bodnar, Benjamin. "Inventory of Conflict and Environment: Panama Canal." May 10, 2006. http://www1.american.edu/ted/ice/panama-canal.htm.

Bogdanich, Walt, Jacqueline Williams, and Ana Graciela Méndez. "The New Panama Canal: A Risky Bet." *New York Times,* June 21, 2016.

Burns, James MacGregor. *Transforming Leadership: A New Pursuit of Happiness*. New York: Grove, 2003.

Espino, Ovidio Diaz. *How Wall Street Created a Nation: J.P. Morgan, Teddy Roosevelt, and the Panama Canal*. New York: Four Walls Eight Windows, 2001.

"Expanded Panama Canal Opens to Cloudy Shipping Future." NOLA.com, June 26, 2016. http://www.nola.com/business/index.ssf/2016/06/expanded_panama_canal_opens_to.html.

Greene, Julie. *The Canal Builders: Making America's Empire at the Panama Canal*. New York: Penguin, 2009.

"Interview with Chad Greene." E-mail interview. Sept. 28, 2016.

Jervis, Rick. "The $5.4 Billion HOV Lane: Will Panama Canal Expansion Boost Global Trade?" *USA Today,* June 25, 2016.

Matalon, Lorne. "Panama Canal Expansion Spurs Environmental Debate." *National Geographic*, June 27, 2007. http://news.nationalgeographic.com/news/2007/06/070627-panama-canal_2.html.

Maurer, Noel, and Carlos Yu. *The Big Ditch: How America Took, Built, Ran, and Ultimately Gave Away the Panama Canal*. Princeton, NJ: Princeton UP, 2011.

Morris, David Z. "Panama Canal Expansion Opens Tomorrow." *Fortune*, June 24, 2016. http://fortune.com/2016/06/25/panama-canal-expansion/.

"The Panama Canal: Now for the Next 100 Years." *The Economist*, August 10, 2014. http://www.economist.com/news/americas/21612185-it-was-good-investment-america-now-china-has-its-eye-canal-now-next-100.

"Theodore Roosevelt and the Panama Canal." PBS. Retrieved October 21, 2016. http://www.pbs.org/wgbh/americanexperience/features/general-article/tr-panama/.

Van Wagtendonk, Anya. "How the Panama Canal Helped Make the U.S. a World Power." PBS, August 15, 2014. http://www.pbs.org/newshour/updates/panama-canal-helped-make-u-s-world-power/.

Weisman, Alan. *The World Without Us*. New York: Thomas Dunne /St. Martin's, 2007.

Index

Page numbers in **boldface** are illustrations. Entries in **boldface** are glossary terms.

About the Author

Tatiana Ryckman is a writer, editor, and teacher from Cleveland, Ohio. She received a master's degree in creative writing from Vermont College of Fine Arts and currently lives in Austin, Texas. Her publications include biographies of Oprah Winfrey and Alexander Hamilton, a book on the economy of the Middle East, and a collection of short stories. When she is not writing, she enjoys eating tacos, reading, and bicycling with friends.